IT'S TIME TO LEARN ABOUT CHICKENS

It's Time to Learn about Chickens

Walter the Educator

Silent King Books
A WhichHead Entertainment Imprint

Copyright © 2025 by Walter the Educator

All rights reserved. No part of this book may be reproduced in any manner whatsoever without written per- mission except in the case of brief quotations embodied in critical articles and reviews.

First Printing, 2024

Disclaimer

This book is a literary work; the story is not about specific persons, locations, situations, and/or circumstances unless mentioned in a historical context. Any resemblance to real persons, locations, situations, and/or circumstances is coincidental. This book is for entertainment and informational purposes only. The author and publisher offer this information without warranties expressed or implied. No matter the grounds, neither the author nor the publisher will be accountable for any losses, injuries, or other damages caused by the reader's use of this book. The use of this book acknowledges an understanding and acceptance of this disclaimer.

It's Time to Learn about Chickens is a collectible early learning book by Walter the Educator suitable for all ages belonging to Walter the Educator's Time to Eat Book Series. Collect more books at WaltertheEducator.com

USE THE EXTRA SPACE TO TAKE NOTES AND DOCUMENT YOUR MEMORIES

CHICKENS

A chicken clucks and struts around,

It's Time to Learn about
Chickens

It pecks the dirt and scrapes the ground.

With feathers bright, white, black, or red,

It bobs its funny little head!

A rooster crows to start the day,

He wakes the farm in his own way.

"Cock-a-doodle-doo!" he sings,

Flapping strong and spreading wings.

A hen lays eggs so smooth and round,

Inside the nest, so safe and sound.

She keeps them warm, she doesn't roam,

Until her chicks are ready to come home!

When eggs hatch open, peep peep peep!

Tiny chicks jump up from sleep.

They're fluffy, yellow, soft, and small,

And follow Mama when she calls!

It's Time to Learn about
Chickens

Chickens love to scratch and peck,

Searching food around the deck.

Seeds and bugs, they love to eat,

With busy feet that never cheat!

Their wings aren't made for flying high,

Just little flutters to the sky.

They flap and hop, then land back down,

Scratching dirt upon the ground.

Their combs and wattles, red and bright,

Help them stay both cool and light.

On sunny days or in the shade,

They strut around, so unafraid.

They huddle close when nights turn cold,

With feathers thick and soft to hold.

Together, safe inside their coop,

It's Time to Learn about
Chickens

They cuddle up, a sleepy group!

On farms or yards, they love to roam,

But always know the way back home.

At sunset time, they walk with care,

And settle in their nesting lair.

So if you hear a cluck or two,

That's just the chickens saying "Hello" to you!

With eggs and feathers, peeps and play,

It's Time to Learn about
Chickens

They brighten up the farm each day!

ABOUT THE CREATOR

Walter the Educator is one of the pseudonyms for Walter Anderson. Formally educated in Chemistry, Business, and Education, he is an educator, an author, a diverse entrepreneur, and he is the son of a disabled war veteran. "Walter the Educator" shares his time between educating and creating. He holds interests and owns several creative projects that entertain, enlighten, enhance, and educate, hoping to inspire and motivate you. Follow, find new works, and stay up to date with Walter the Educator™

at WaltertheEducator.com

www.ingramcontent.com/pod-product-compliance
Lightning Source LLC
LaVergne TN
LVHW051920060526
838201LV00060B/4089